Summer to Summer. Looking

Gill McEvoy

Cinnamon Press
:: small miracles from distinctive voices ::

Published by Cinnamon Press
www.cinnamonpress.com

ISBN 978-1-78864-181-4

British Library Cataloguing in Publication Data. A CIP record for this book can be obtained from the British Library.

Designed and typeset in Bodoni by Cinnamon Press. Cover design by Adam Craig.

Cinnamon Press is represented by Inpress Ltd.

Acknowledgements

My thanks to the editors of the following magazines for publishing some of these poems: *Spelt, Strix, Birmingham Poetry Journal, Orbis, Ink sweat and tears, The Frogmore Papers, Sidhe Press, Artemis, Wivenhoe Poetry, Obsessed with Pipework*, and *Poetry Breakfast*.

'Red Magnolias' won runner-up prize in Wirral Poetry Festival's Competition.

About the Author

Gill McEvoy is a Hawthornden Fellow. Her first pamphlet, *Uncertain Days*, (Happenstance Press 2006) earned a special mention in the PBS bulletin. Her third pamphlet, *The First Telling*, (Happenstance Press 2014) won the 2015 Michael marks Award. She has two full collections from Cinnamon Press: *The Plucking Shed*, 2010 and *Rise*, 2013. Also two collections from Hedgehog Press: *Are You Listening?* 2020, and *Selected Poems*, 2024. She lives in Devon, where she runs a monthly poetry reading group, and is a regular member of Company of Poets in Totnes. Gill cares deeply about wildlife and works with a group called Bee-wild, planting flowers and shrubs around her village for the benefit of bees and other pollinators, and thereby giving pleasure also to passers-by!

Contents

*All those who care about the natural world,
especially to my friends in Bee-wild*

Summer to Summer, Looking

The Bird by the River

It remained on the blackened root
above the river's wild race and did not move.

I stayed in place, watching,
very still.

Eventually I heard it start to sing:
plain notes and then the thinnest trill.

The usual group of people walking dogs
passed by and asked what I was staring at.

I pointed, but they thought it just a leaf
bleached by autumn, and walked on.

I despaired of ignorance; I knew
the dipper and I was right: when it flew,

the bright moon
of its small breast shone like snow.

Drought

Sun rises from its blood-streaked bed,
climbs the hot metal of a blinding sky,
burns the grass, scorches earth.

Animals in fields seek whatever shade there is.
Flames take hold of dried-out edges.
Trees drop their leaves.

Everywhere sere and parched;
cancer burns through skin, through bone.
Things wither in the baking heat.

When the hot moon shows its face
it too is merciless in blaze and glare.

We beg and pray for rain
but the sun goes on
burning, burning.

Tree at Dusk

What was this tree?
We picked a leaf, sierra-edged like beech,
and counted veins: eleven at least,
surely this was more than those of beech?

We hadn't quite decided when,
high up in the canopy, the last of sunset
lit up the strings of those pagoda roofs
that house the seed,
those hanging lanterns masterly in shape,
each one bracketing a smaller one below,
cascading down.

It was hornbeam
we were standing underneath:
'Beam', Old English for tree
from German 'Baum';
and 'horn' for anything that's hard.

A tree that gives us mallets, skittles,
Butchers' blocks and wheel spokes.
Hornbeam, no mistake at all.

October Forecast

Heavy fronts of dahlias and fallen fruit,
sharp stars, huge moons,
cold mornings, condensation,
slow moving wasps and bluebottles,
occasional red admirals,
patches of chrysanthemum
and aster flowers,
shorter days, colder nights,
leaf fall, intermittent rain,
mist clearing later in the day.

In the Snowdrop Woods

The ground is dry. Mid-November.
No sign of them now.

But months ago, after weeks of rain
so heavy the paths turned to
boot-wrenching mud,
I saw them.

Snowdrops swarmed up every bank,
crammed every hidden hollow,
smothered the edges of the path
and lit the river's bank.

I found myself snow-blind
in their blizzard of white.
And I forgot the mud.

At Stover

the Devon poetry trail of Ted Hughes' work

The kids don't want to read
the poems on the boards,
nor to hear them read aloud.

They want to hide-and-seek
among the trees, ride horses
on the fallen logs.

Anyway, they say,
that wildlife in those poems
is hiding 'cos it's freezing!

(Even we who came specifically
to honour Hughes and read his words,
are chilled from so much standing still.)

Out on the lake two crested grebes
are paddling, crowned heads held
like hieroglyphics in the air.

We find them so much easier to read.

The Pine Tree

The inside of its bark is red,
its heartwood is red;
when a branch is cut
the wound is red
yet it weeps,
not blood,
but thick white tears.

February Afternoon

Outside a blackbird,
mistaking this mild weather
for spring, is singing.

By the pond dry reeds
consider cranking into life
from black mud at their roots.

Spathes of arum
cock their green ears to the wind,
catkins fatten on the willow trees.

In the garden hellebores
hang their heads inside
their cabin of leaves.

Snow is forecast on the radio.

The Mersey Estuary

Time here marked
by the turn of tide,
advance and retreat
of wading birds,
bait diggers,
the slow revolution
of turbine blades.

A place of silt,
soft mud,
slippery surfaces.
And light -
light
like a great sail
shaking out dazzle.

Not a place this
of soft earth
under leaf fall,
not home.

But strange.
Rare.
Beautiful.

Pruning the Wisteria

With my secateurs and saw
I've clubbed you into ugliness.

This butchered row of blunted paws,
if I have got the pruning right,

will turn in May to
lavish spills of purple.

Drunken bees will drool
among your fragrant blooms.

Until then, this is how you'll be—
sullen, unappealing—

and I might feel
half sorry for my cruelty.

Of All We Looked at in March 2020

onion-dome buds on the sycamore,
green and fattening,
mahogany spears of buds on the beech,
the dusky blues of the alder catkins,
the triple crown of buds
that mark the finial of ash twigs,
a trinity St Patrick might have used,

it's the space
between the dark buds of the beech
that we remember now,
their perfect skill at social distancing.

Haunting the Pool by the Bridge

We were sure this pool, overhung
by willows, brambles, wild rose,
would be the habitat of kingfisher.

Sometimes on our way here we saw a dipper,
once a deer drinking at the river's edge.

But never that un-nerving shock of blue,
that compact bullet streaking by so fast

it leaves you wondering
did you see it/ did you not?

We were like pilgrims clinging
to a worn-out faith,

trusting that the longed-for vision
would reveal itself one day
and fill our hearts with radiance,

knowing deep inside ourselves
it never would.

Red Magnolias

Brazen flaunters
in their scarlet gowns,
they're gaudy Southern Belles
lusting for adulation,
greedy for ground.

Across the village green
the modest English trees
stand back,
protected by a line of posts
from these brash Medusa heads,

these puffed-up cobras rising
from their basketry of twig.

Window Seat

You leave the comfort of the Raeburn,
pass through the hall where the chill
grabs you in its icy grip,
up to this room where books line every wall
and stand in columns on the rug.
An iron latch, plain wooden door,
and a window seat, cushions and curtains
patterned with fruit.

It is not the room but what it meets
when you draw the curtains back.

You take a blanket from the bed,
snuggle in the window seat to watch,
in the grey and misty April dawn,
the wood outside where an owl
might squat on a dripping branch, at roost,
or folded in the undergrowth, a deer at rest;
certainly a fox, at daybreak,
trotting home with nothing in its mouth.

Dandelions

arrive in hordes
for the Festival of the Returning Sun,
pitch their tents on every verge,
daub the grass
with oily brash of yellow.

When the celebration's over
parasols of white
in thousands
litter the empty site.

'To Watch a Cloud is Consoling. Always.'

Jaan Kaaplinski, from In the Forest

You sent me a cloud when I was ill.
It would have my name on it, you said,
so I would know it instantly.

I watched the window from my bed,
studying clouds.

One afternoon
of white and navy cumuli
it came:
a grey horse resting in a field.

This was the one you meant, I knew—
I watched its body gently yield
from horse to cloud again as such shapes do.

Each day it floats beside me now,
that quiet horse, your gift. My cloud.

Dealing with the Straying Sheep at the Holiday Cottage

When a sheep got into the garden
you went out in the dark alone
to urge it through the fence,
then used a wheelbarrow
to block the gap.

When you came back,
shoes and ankles soaked,
nettle stings
on the pale skin of your legs,
a kind of glory lit your face.

You stripped off shoes and socks,
walked about the kitchen
in your wet bare feet.

Shining prints of night-dew
marked your passage there.

Carp and Lilies

Water-lilies are
opening on the lake,
their buds arranged
among the flat spread leaves
like fat pears on a plate.

Slowly the petals separate,
hold up white cups
to a sky of blue.

Curious carp swim up,
mouths pursed
like unripe plums,
imitate the blooms
in a lily gape of throat,
barbells trailing from their lips

like anthers in the
water's gloom.

Bumble Bee Summer

The alder-buckthorn tree is singing
with the sound
of working bees;

I watch their plump black trundle
flower-to-flower
among the leaves.

The carder and the meadow bee
squeeze
up monkshood's deep blue sleeves

The carpenter and garden bees,
the masonry, the solitary,
probe the hoods of lamium.

The red-tailed
and the buff-tailed bees
cling to the face of dark geranium.

Long hot summer, good summer,
loud with
the industry of bumble bees.

Racing the Harvest Moon down the Motorway

A sudden stretch of empty motorway.

I put my foot down hard to beat
the moon
to the exit I am looking for.

We roar along, the moon and I,
exulting in the silver broadway
of the road.

Engine throbbing, needle climbing,
who could resist
this moment's recklessness?

Then a barn-owl filters from a hedge,
its white face round as moon,
its huge eyes dark as caution.

I slow down.

The moon,
always a good sport,
slows down too.